ILLINOIS

HELLO
U.S.A.

by Kathy P. Anderson

Lerner Publications Company

You'll find this picture of a field of corn and soybeans at the beginning of each chapter. Farms cover much of Illinois, and corn and soybeans are the state's leading crops. In fact, enough corn is grown in the state each year to fill 460,000 swimming pools. And enough soybeans are grown in Illinois each year to fill 118,000 school buses!

Cover (left): Chicago skyline. Cover (right): Cornfield near Springfield. Pages 2-3: Abraham Lincoln's home in Springfield. Page 3: Sculpture at Illinois Center Building in Chicago.

This book is available in two editions:
Library binding by Lerner Publications Company, a division of Lerner Publishing Group
Soft cover by First Avenue Editions, an imprint of Lerner Publishing Group
241 First Avenue North
Minneapolis, MN 55401 U.S.A.

Website address: www.lernerbooks.com

Library of Congress Cataloging-in-Publication Data

Anderson, Kathy P., 1958–
    Illinois / by Kathy P. Anderson (Revised and expanded 2ⁿᵈ edition)
      p.   cm. — (Hello U.S.A.)
    Includes index.
    ISBN: 0–8225–4054–1 (lib. bdg. : alk. paper)
    ISBN: 0–8225–4154–8 (pbk. : alk. paper)
    1. Illinois—Juvenile literature. [1. Illinois.] I. Title. II. Series.
    F541.3.A53 2002
    977.3—dc21   2001001161

Manufactured in the United States of America
1 2 3 4 5 6 – JR – 07 06 05 04 03 02

CONTENTS

The Sears Tower dominates the skyline of Chicago.

The Prairie State

n the midwestern United States lies Illinois, the Prairie State. Cornfields and pastures stretch for miles across Illinois's long horizon. In the northeastern corner, skyscrapers taller than the tallest hills in the state break the horizon. The buildings are part of Chicago, the third largest city in the United States.

Some people think that Chicago is Illinois. This sprawling urban area dwarfs the cities and towns around it. But there is much more to the state than its largest city.

Illinois hosts an interesting blend of city and country living.

ILLINOIS
Political Map

⊛ State capital

0   25   50 Miles
0   25   50   75   100 Kilometers

The drawing of Illinois on this page is called a political map. It shows features created by people, including cities, railways, and parks. The map on the facing page is called a physical map. It shows physical features of Illinois, such as coasts, islands, mountains, rivers, and lakes. The colors represent a range of elevations, or heights above sea level (see legend box). This map also shows the geographical regions of Illinois.

Galena
Rockford
Zion
Freeport
Belvidere
Highland Park
Oregon
Sycamore
Wilmette
Grand Detour
Brookfield
Chicago
Aurora
Naperville
Rock Island
Mendota
Moline
Peoria
Normal
Petersburg
⊛ Springfield
Collinsville
Olney
East Saint Louis
Cahokia
Freeburg
Mount Vernon
Du Quoin
Shawneetown
Shawnee National Forest
Cobden
Metropolis

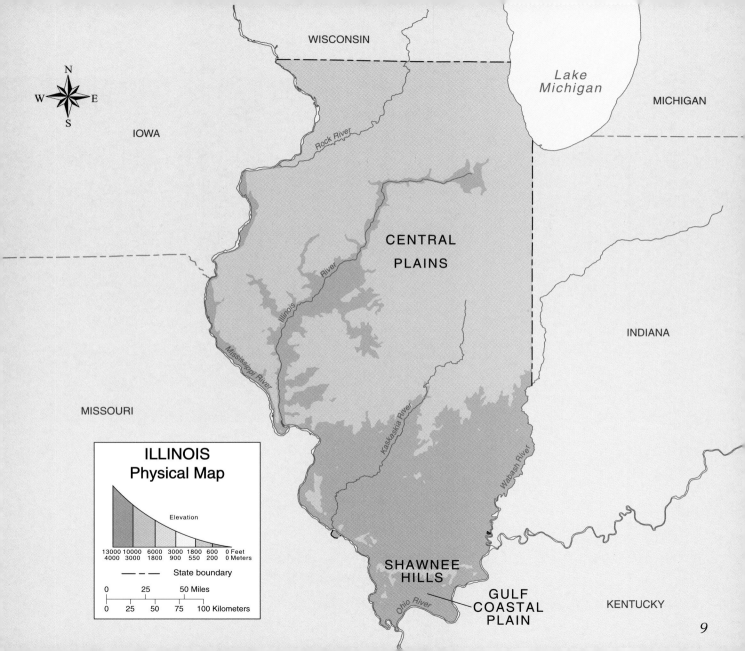

WISCONSIN

Lake
Michigan

MICHIGAN

IOWA

Rock River

CENTRAL
PLAINS

Illinois River

Mississippi River

INDIANA

MISSOURI

Kaskaskia River

Wabash River

SHAWNEE
HILLS

GULF
COASTAL
PLAIN

Ohio River

KENTUCKY

ILLINOIS
Physical Map

Elevation

13000	10000	6000	3000	1800	600	0 Feet
4000	3000	1800	900	550	200	0 Meters

- - - State boundary

0		25		50 Miles

| 0 | 25 | 50 | 75 | 100 Kilometers |

9

In western Illinois, farmland and forests line the mighty Mississippi.

Water hems in much of Illinois. Lake Michigan—one of the five **Great Lakes**—laps against the state's northeastern corner. Along western Illinois, the Mississippi River carves a squiggly boundary. The Ohio River flows along southern Illinois, and the Wabash River marks part of the state's edge in the east.

Water, in the form of **glaciers,** also shaped Illinois's largest land region—the Central Plains. Glaciers, or huge sheets of ice, crept over most of the area thousands of years ago, flattening the land in their path. When the glaciers melted, they left ground-up rock and clay, which became the rich soil of the Central Plains.

The flat, fertile plains of the region stretch from Illinois's northern border almost to its southern tip. At one time the region was a **prairie** (grassland), but in modern times most of it is planted with corn and soybeans. The northwestern corner of the Central Plains, untouched by glaciers, has rolling hills and valleys. Rich deposits of coal lie in the southwestern half of the region.

A large part of Illinois is flat and covered with cornfields.

The Shawnee Hills region of Illinois is hilly and rocky.

The glaciers stopped before they reached the Shawnee Hills, a region just south of the Central Plains. Nature lovers enjoy the deep valleys, steep riverbanks, and forested hills of this strip of land.

The very southern tip of Illinois includes part of the Gulf Coastal Plain, a large region that extends south all the way to the Gulf of Mexico (an arm of the Atlantic Ocean). Hills mark the northern section of Illinois's Gulf Coastal Plain, while the southern part is flat and swampy.

Illinois has about 500 waterways. The Illinois River, the longest inside the state, runs southwest into the Mississippi River. The Kaskaskia River in the south and the Rock River in the north also flow into the Mississippi.

Cypress trees grow
in Horseshoe Lake,
located in the
Gulf Coastal Plain.

Lake Michigan touches the northeastern corner of Illinois. The lake is linked to the Saint Lawrence Seaway, which connects the Great Lakes to the Atlantic Ocean. Illinoisans send products from Lake Michigan along the seaway to the ocean and around the world. Because Chicago is connected to these important waterways, the city has become one of the nation's busiest ports.

Chicago's port on Lake Michigan is a destination for ships from all over the world.

Many Illinoisans explore their state's woodlands in search of wildflowers.

Illinois's weather changes swiftly from day to day and from season to season. Cold winds from the north and warm winds from the south often sweep over the state's flat plains, making temperatures drop or rise quickly. Summer temperatures average 75° F in the north, but in the south, temperatures average more than 80° F. In the winter, temperatures in the north usually drop below 25° F, while they stay around 36° F in the south.

During the spring and summer, tornadoes and thunderstorms often threaten cities and farmlands throughout Illinois. In 1917 Illinois was hit by one of the longest-lasting tornadoes in history. While most tornadoes usually last less than an hour, this one lasted seven hours.

In wooded areas throughout Illinois, deer, rabbits, squirrels, raccoon, and foxes live and raise their young. Muskrat, beavers, mink, and otters build their homes and find food near the state's rivers and lakes.

Ducks and geese from the northern states and Canada pass through Illinois as they fly south for the winter and north again for the summer. The Illinois River valley is a rest area for about 2 million ducks.

Illinois's forests are full of wild animals like raccoons.

From Prairies to Skyscrapers

The first people to live in what later became Illinois probably moved into the area about 12,000 years ago. These Native Americans, or American Indians, moved from place to place, hunting large animals and gathering plants for food. Around 300 B.C., another group of Native Americans came to the region. These people are known as mound builders.

The mound builders got their name from the huge earthen mounds they made. They buried their dead in some of the mounds and built temples on top of others. Important people, such as priests and chiefs, lived in the temples.

Scientists have learned about what life was like for the mound builders by studying their skeletons.

The settlement at Cahokia was one of the most sophisticated prehistoric civilizations in North America north of Mexico.

The Indians built their largest village near what would become Cahokia, Illinois. With a population of about 40,000, this village was really a city. It had a central mound, which was like the downtown area of modern cities. Surrounding this mound were five "suburbs," or clusters of wood-and-grass houses where most of the people lived. The village farmers grew corn, beans, and squash, while skilled craftspeople made pottery, mirrors, cups, and jewelry.

By A.D. 1400, the mound builders had disappeared. No one knows for certain, but they may have been wiped out by diseases or repeated crop failures.

Soon several tribes—including the Cahokia, Kaskaskia, Michigamea, Moingwena, Peoria, and Tamarou—moved into the region. These tribes were known as the Illinois, a French spelling of the Indians' word for "people." (Other tribes, including the Sauk, the Ottawa, and the Winnebago, would later inhabit the area.)

During dry summers, prairie fires sometimes swept through the Illinois Indians' homes in the Central Plains.

The Illinois lived in villages near river valleys. They made canoes, houses, and tools from wood. In the spring, the women planted fields of corn and beans. In the winter, the tribes left their villages to hunt buffalo.

To catch the buffalo, the Illinois sometimes surrounded a herd with a ring of fire. The hunters then shot the trapped animals with bows and arrows. The Illinois ate the buffalo meat and made the skins into clothes and blankets.

The Illinois probably first met white people in 1673, when French explorers Louis Jolliet and Jacques Marquette traveled through the region. The explorers' trip took them down the Mississippi River and up the Illinois River to Lake Michigan.

France soon claimed the land that Jolliet and Marquette had visited, and French fur traders set up trading posts. The traders gave European goods, such as iron tools and glass beads, to the Illinois in exchange for beaver pelts. Traders made lots of money by selling the pelts in Europe, where men's hats made of beaver skins were very popular.

Marquette *(standing)*, a Catholic priest, and Jolliet *(front)*, a fur trader, may have been the first white people to explore the Mississippi and Illinois Rivers.

Like the French, the British wanted the land and rich fur trade in North America for themselves. In 1754, the French and the British fought for control of North America in what became known as the French and Indian War. During the war, the Illinois and many neighboring tribes helped the French fight the British. But even with help from the Indians, the French lost the war and left the region.

Chicago in 1779
(Then Called Eschikago)

Jean Baptiste Pointe du Sable, a black fur trader, is considered the founder of Chicago. He built a trading post near an Indian camp on the Chicago River in 1779.

The Indians were soon pushed out of the region as well. The United States claimed the Illinois area in 1783. By the early 1800s, settlers were coming down the Ohio River from Kentucky, Virginia, and other states.

The population of settlers was soon large enough for Illinois to qualify for statehood. On December 3, 1818, Illinois became the twenty-first state. Politicians from Illinois asked the U.S. government to move the new state's northern border 60 miles farther north. The extended border brought a small community—Chicago—into the new state. If the border had not been moved, Chicago would be in Wisconsin.

More newcomers arrived. The state's population tripled in 10 years, reaching 150,000 by 1830. Although the new settlers and U.S. troops pushed most Native Americans westward, some Indians remained in Illinois. Black Hawk, a Sauk chief and warrior, knew that his tribe had been forced to give up its land unfairly. He and his followers refused to leave their village.

Followers of Black Hawk flee during the Battle of Bad Axe. U.S. troops killed almost 300 of Black Hawk's supporters as they tried to surrender.

The U.S. Army prepared to drive the group out of Illinois in 1832. Warriors from neighboring tribes, including the Kickapoo, Potawatomi, and Fox, joined the Sauk to fight the army in what became known as the Black Hawk War. The Native

Americans were outnumbered and beaten badly in the four-month-long war. By the war's end, settlers and the U.S. government claimed all the land in Illinois.

In the 1830s and 1840s, thousands of new settlers came to Illinois. Most came from Europe and the eastern United States, where jobs and farmland were hard to find. Some of the new-comers dug canals. Others mined coal in the southern half of the state. Many built farms and planted corn in the prairie soil of central Illinois.

John Deere invented the steel plow in 1837 in Grand Detour, Illinois. This plow could cut through thick prairie sod, allowing farmers to plant more crops.

These farmers profited when the Illinois and Michigan Canal opened in 1848. The canal connected Lake Michigan to the Illinois and Mississippi Rivers. Farmers in central and southern Illinois could send their crops and livestock cheaply and quickly by water to Chicago. From there the crops were shipped across the Great Lakes to the large markets of the East Coast. Returning

Farmers from central and southern Illinois sent their grain to Chicago. There, the grain was cleaned and temporarily stored in grain elevators.

boats carried lumber, manufactured goods, and farm machinery to Chicago. The goods were then sent to Illinois's farmers.

Even as the canal opened, railroad crews were hammering train tracks into place. By the early 1850s, Illinois had thousands of miles of railroad tracks. Trains brought coal from southern Illinois to Chicago. The coal was then burned to fuel machines in the city's factories.

The railroads also brought Irish, German, and other European **immigrants** to the state. Many immigrants built farms, but others moved to cities. These newcomers, who often came to the country with little money, were usually willing to work for low wages.

This cheap labor pool, as well as good transportation and a cheap source of coal nearby, helped industries in Chicago to boom. Cattle and hogs from Illinois's farms were transported to Chicago's stockyards, where the animals were fattened and then butchered. Illinois's farmers also sent their corn to Chicago, where it was weighed and stored in grain elevators. The meat and grain were shipped from Chicago by boat or train to eastern markets.

Chicago's lumberyards bought trees from Wisconsin, then cut the timber into boards and sold it to

Chicago was home to many lumberyards. Boards, as well as bricks, were used to build houses and pave streets in growing cities like Chicago.

the city's furniture factories. The factories sent the finished furniture to farms and towns west of the Mississippi River.

While Illinois and other Northern states earned money making goods in factories, the Southern states relied on farming for their money. Many Southern farmers used slaves to work the land. Southern politicians argued that this was the only way Southern farmers could make a profit.

But in Northern states such as Illinois, slavery was illegal. Many people wanted to outlaw slavery in every state. Southerners feared that one of those people was Abraham Lincoln, an Illinoisan who was elected U.S. president in 1860.

Abraham Lincoln

Soon after Lincoln's election, the Southern states decided to form a new country—the Confederate States of America—where slavery would remain legal. In 1861 President Lincoln sent Union, or Northern, troops to keep the United Sates together. The Civil War had begun. In Illinois, factories made weapons and farmers grew food for Union soldiers, who won the war in 1865.

The Lincoln-Douglas Debates

In 1854 Senator Stephen Douglas of Illinois introduced the Kansas-Nebraska Act. This law allowed settlers in the western United States to decide whether they wanted slavery to be legal in their territories. Many people were afraid that this act would allow slavery to spread throughout the west.

Abraham Lincoln, a lawyer from Springfield, Illinois, agreed with these people. In 1858 he ran against Douglas for a seat in the U.S. Senate. The two men argued about slavery in a series of debates, or discussions, held in seven Illinois towns. Lincoln lost the election, but he proved himself a great speaker. He became so famous for his strong arguments against slavery that he was chosen to run for U.S. president in 1860. This time he won.

Political cartoons of the day depicted the rivalry between Abraham Lincoln *(right)* and Stephen Douglas *(left)*.

30

After the Civil War, more factories were built all over Illinois, creating many new jobs. Immigrants from Poland, Italy, and other European countries moved to Chicago, where they found jobs making candy, soap, and iron and steel. By 1870, Chicago's population had grown to 300,000. It was the world's largest market for grain, livestock, and lumber.

When immigrants came to Chicago, they usually moved into neighborhoods with people from their native country.

The Great Chicago Fire

The summer of 1871 was the driest in Chicago's history. Wood buildings and wood sidewalks were all dry as a bone. So when a cow owned by Mrs. Patrick O'Leary kicked over an oil lamp on October 8, 1871, the fire that started in the cow's barn spread quickly to nearby homes. It didn't take long for it to flame out of control. The fire burned so brightly that the sky was as light as day. A blizzard of burning sparks flew from the fire, lighting small fires wherever they landed and blistering animals and people. The air around the fire was so hot that houses burst into flames before the fire even reached them. The Great Chicago Fire destroyed 2,000 acres of the city, left more than 100,000 people homeless, and reduced $200 million worth of property to ashes. Only two public buildings—the water tower and the pumping station—survived the fire.

Coal from southern Illinois was sent by rail *(left)* to industries such as the stockyards *(below)* of East Saint Louis and Chicago.

East Saint Louis, Illinois, became the site of giant steel-making and oil-cleaning factories. In Joliet, Moline, and Rock Island, workers built farm machines that helped farmers raise more crops.

Many of the factory workers, especially in Chicago, worked long hours for low pay. Sometimes they worked under dangerous conditions. In addition, many workers could only afford to live in cramped buildings of poor quality.

In 1886, a group of factory workers in Chicago went on strike. They refused to go to work in order to protest their poor working conditions and long hours. At a large gathering of workers in Haymarket Square, a bomb exploded, and violence broke out. Seven policemen and at least four workers were killed at what became known as the Haymarket Riot.

After this, conditions began to improve slowly for workers, immigrants, and the poor in Illinois. Working hours were made shorter, factories became less dangerous, and programs to improve housing and education were started.

Chicago continued to grow. By 1890, it was the second-largest city in the United States (after New York City), with over 1 million people. In fact, Chicago earned the nickname "Second City."

In the early years of the 1900s, many black people living in southern states began moving north to Chicago. They had heard of jobs there. Black communities in Chicago and other cities in Illinois began to grow.

When World War I started in Europe in 1914, factories in Illinois operated at full speed to make weapons and tanks. There was so much to do that more workers were needed.

More and more black people from southern states moved north. Chicago's black population soon tripled. Because whites would not sell homes or rent apartments in much of the city to blacks, most black people squeezed into a few small, rundown neighborhoods. After the war ended in 1918, African Americans continued to arrive in Chicago, looking for jobs. But they were usually offered the lowest-paying jobs in the city.

Black communities sprang up in Chicago and other cities in Illinois. There was sometimes tension between white and black people. In the early 1900s, there were riots in Springfield, East Saint Louis, and Chicago.

Prohibition, a set of laws that made the producing and selling of liquor a crime, was passed in 1920. Gangsters in Chicago became rich and powerful by supplying liquor to the city's 20,000 illegal bars, called **speakeasies.** Gangsters also operated illegal gambling parlors. Al Capone was one of the most famous of Chicago's gangsters. Capone was arrested in 1936, just three years after Prohibition ended. But many gangsters remained powerful for years to come.

During Prohibition, gangsters competed with each other—often violently—for control of the liquor market. In the Saint Valentine's Day massacre, the era's most famous shoot-out, gangsters dressed as police killed seven members of a rival gang.

During the Great Flood of 1937, the Ohio River overflowed, leaving eight counties in southern Illinois underwater. Places like Shawneetown *(above)* were devastated by the flood.

This Illinois factory made vehicles called earth movers for soldiers in Europe during World War II.

In 1941 U.S. troops went to war in Europe. During World War II, Illinois's factories were busier than ever before. In Chicago, Rockford, Moline, Peoria, Springfield, and East Saint Louis, workers made planes, bombs, tanks, and other goods needed for the war. Farmers sent tons of grain overseas to feed the soldiers.

After the war, manufacturing continued to grow. But the number of farms dropped by half, as farmers left their fields for higher-paying jobs in factories.

From the 1950s through the 1970s, politics in Chicago and the rest of Illinois were influenced by

Chicago's powerful mayor, Richard J. Daley. Daley controlled the Chicago government tightly. He made sure that his friends and supporters got jobs in the city and state governments, even if they weren't honest. During his time in office, he reorganized Chicago's police department, encouraged companies to build skyscrapers downtown, and tried to improve housing for the city's poor.

By the 1970s, many factories and other businesses began leaving Illinois for states where companies could be run more cheaply. In Chicago, people with enough money moved to the suburbs, leaving behind the city's crime, run-down neighborhoods, and overcrowded schools.

During the 1990s, Illinois's factories began growing again. High-technology companies were attracted to the state. But in the 2000s, Illinois still faces problems such as high rates of poverty in urban areas and declining farm prices. As many Illinoisans prosper, the state must try to balance the needs of all of its people, from the inner city to the farm.

Harold Washington, Chicago's first African American mayor, served from 1983 until his death in 1987.

PEOPLE & ECONOMY

A Rich Heritage

Of the more than 12 million people in Illinois, more than half live in or around Chicago. Rows of skyscrapers line the city's downtown. Beyond Chicago, though, Illinois takes on a different look. Tractors replace commuter trains, and skyscrapers become stalks of corn. There are other cities in Illinois, too. Of these, Rockford, Aurora, Springfield, Peoria, and Naperville are the biggest.

Some Illinoisans live in small towns like Cobden *(left)* in southwestern Illinois. But more than 6 million of the state's residents live in or near Chicago. Chinatown *(opposite page)* is one of Chicago's many ethnic neighborhoods.

41

Two young Illinois
artists work outdoors.

In Illinois, about 15 percent of the people are African American, 12 percent are Hispanic, and 3 percent are Asian. Almost everyone else in the state has ancestors from Ireland, Poland, Russia, Germany, Italy, Sweden, and other European countries.

When Illinois became a state, almost all Illinoisans were farmers. Though more than three-fourths of Illinois's land is still used for agriculture, less than 2 percent of Illinoisans work on farms, and farmers earn only 2 percent of the state's money.

More corn is grown in the state than any other crop. Illinois is one of the top soybean producers in the nation. Other crops include wheat, oats, and sorghum (a cereal grain). Farmers in northern Illinois plant asparagus, beans, and cabbage. Many farmers also raise hogs, sheep, and cattle. Mining earns less than 1 percent of the state's money. In the southern half of Illinois, about 40 million tons of coal are dug up every year.

Sheep cluster around a farmer during feeding time.

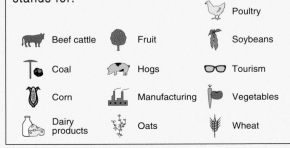

ILLINOIS
Economic Map

The symbols on this map show where different economic activities take place in Illinois. The legend below explains what each symbol stands for.

		Poultry
Beef cattle	Fruit	Soybeans
Coal	Hogs	Tourism
Corn	Manufacturing	Vegetables
Dairy products	Oats	Wheat

Illinois earns 19 percent of its money from manufacturing. Many Illinoisans build machines that are used all over the world. Moline and Peoria have some of the world's biggest manufacturers of farm and construction equipment. Factories in Normal and Belvidere produce cars, and factories in Freeport and Mount Vernon make tires.

Other manufacturers in the state process crops and livestock into food products such as breakfast cereal, sausage, and candy. In the Chicago area, people package medicines and cleaning solutions. Illinoisans also print books and newspapers. The largest printing company in the United States is in Chicago.

In a factory in Moline, workers put together a large tractor.

Illinois sells many of its products throughout the world. More goods are bought and sold at the Chicago Board of Trade than anywhere else in the world. Buyers and sellers in Chicago trade millions of tons of grain, cattle, eggs, coal, oil, and other products each year. Truck drivers, train engineers, ship captains, and airplane pilots move tons of crops, coal, and manufactured goods from Illinois to markets outside the state.

Pushed by a tugboat, a barge floats down the Illinois River.

Firefighters, some of Illinois's government workers, save lives and help keep the state safe.

People who trade or transport goods are called service workers because they provide a service to other people or businesses. About two-thirds of all working Illinoisans have some kind of service job, including nurses, salespeople, and bankers. Some service workers sell tickets and move luggage at Chicago-O'Hare International Airport, the world's busiest airfield. Every 30 seconds, one plane lands and another departs there. About 12 percent of Illinoisans work for the government.

When Illinoisans aren't working, many of them like to go swimming, fishing, or boating on the state's lakes and rivers. Chicagoans play on the beaches along Lake Michigan and bicycle and picnic in the city's parks. Many Illinoisans hike over the hills and through the valleys of the Shawnee National Forest in southern Illinois.

Fans of the Chicago Cubs enjoy a sunny day at Wrigley Field.

Baseball fans cheer for one of Illinois's two major league teams—the Chicago White Sox, who play at Comiskey Park, and the Chicago Cubs, who play at Wrigley Field. Football fans watch the Chicago Bears compete at Soldier Field. The Blackhawks, the professional hockey team, and the Bulls, of the National Basketball Association, both play at the United Center in Chicago.

Illinois boasts many museums and historic sites. Chicago is home to the Art Institute of Chicago, the Museum of Contemporary Art, the Adler Planetarium, and the John G. Shedd Aquarium. Visitors to Chicago can explore a life-size copy of a coal mine at the Museum of Science and Industry and dinosaur skeletons at the Field Museum of Natural History. The DuSable Museum of African American History, one of the finest of its kind in the country, is also in Chicago. In Rockford, the Time Museum displays thousands of clocks, some of which are 3,000 years old.

Visitors can view a timepiece *(above right)* that is over 2,500 years old at the Time Museum in Rockford. The stars come out during the daytime at the Adler Planetarium *(right)* in Chicago.

Galena, a city in northwestern Illinois, has been restored to look as it did in the 1800s, when it was a booming mining town. The Cahokia Mounds near Collinsville and the Black Hawk statue near Oregon remind visitors of Illinois's earliest residents. Monuments to Abraham Lincoln attract tourists to New Salem and to Springfield in central Illinois. Springfield, the state's capital, also hosts the Illinois State Fair every year.

Animal lovers meet an elephant up close at the Brookfield Zoo *(above).* Making soap bubbles is one way visitors to the Kohl Children's Museum in Wilmette *(right)* can learn about science.

Chicago offers a variety of festivals and parades, including the Polish Constitution Day parade, the Chicago Jazz Festival, the Saint Patrick's Day Parade, Taste of Chicago, and Venetian Night. Illinoisans can sample the food at Mendota's Sweet Corn Festival.

Each summer, visitors and residents of Chicago flock to the Taste of Chicago, a two-week festival offering food, music, and fireworks.

THE ENVIRONMENT

Reducing Waste

Illinois has a lot of people for a state its size. Twenty-three states are larger than Illinois, but only four have higher populations. Illinois's many people and the companies they work for need water and land to survive. But the waste created by people and industries threatens these limited natural resources.

Illinois's factories, businesses, and people produce millions of tons of waste every year. People and

Illinois's large population produces a lot of garbage, and residents of cities such as Chicago work hard to keep the city's waterfront *(left)* and streets *(opposite page)* clean.

industry throw out an average of 37,000 tons of **solid waste** each day. Magazines, food, grass cuttings, furniture, used appliances, and packaging material are all solid waste. Most solid waste ends up in **landfills,** places where solid waste is buried. In 1998, 10 percent more trash went into landfills than in 1997.

At this landfill, a bulldozer rearranges waste so that it will take up less space.

Empty landfills are shaped like enormous bathtubs. Waste is dumped into the landfill, packed down, and covered with dirt or a special kind of foam. When rain or snow falls on a landfill, the water mixes with rotting garbage to form a liquid called **leachate.**

At the bottom of most landfills is a liner, usually a huge sheet of plastic with clay underneath it, which keeps the leachate from seeping into the ground. But the liner can crack or split, allowing leachate to leak. The leachate then carries pollutants through the soil under the landfill to **groundwater** and to nearby rivers and lakes. When people or wildlife drink the poisoned water, they can get sick or die.

Even if landfills were completely safe, Illinoisans would still have a garbage problem. Fifty-eight landfills accepted trash in 1998. Only 56 landfills are still active. If no new landfills are built and their use remains constant, the state's existing landfills will be overflowing by 2015. Illinoisans need to find other ways to get rid of their solid waste.

One way to control waste is to reduce the amount of trash produced. For example, people can ask to stop getting magazines, mail-order catalogs, or telephone directories that they don't need. When shopping, people can choose items without lots of cardboard or plastic packaging, so less material will be thrown away.

When these glass bottles are recycled, they will be broken into pieces, melted, and then shaped into new glass forms.

Another way to cut down on waste is to buy goods that can be reused. Rather than buying plastic or paper cups and containers, which are thrown away after one use, people can use glass and ceramic cups and plates. People can also decide to buy one copy of a magazine or newspaper to share with family or friends.

Recycling trash also reduces solid waste. Many scientists think that we could recycle more than 50 percent of all solid waste. But in 1998 only about 28 percent of Illinois's solid waste was recycled. By law, every county in Illinois must recycle at least 25 percent of its waste.

People can choose to buy items packaged in recyclable materials. This encourages manufacturers to package their products in recyclable materials. Glass, aluminum foil, tin cans, paper, and plastic can all be recycled. Food scraps, grass clippings, and leaves can be recycled in a compost pile—a mixture of rotting vegetation that is saved to fertilize soil.

Illinoisans hope to preserve and enjoy their natural areas by cutting down on their trash.

Illinois is working to make less solid waste. In 1990 the state government banned yard waste from landfills. Instead of throwing grass clippings and leaves in the trash, residents must leave them on the lawn or put them in a compost pile. Cities throughout Illinois pick up recyclables—newspapers, cans, and plastic—from homes and businesses. Schools in Illinois are required by law to teach students how to reduce and recycle.

In some towns in Illinois, residents gather leaves in a compost pile. Later, the leaves will be used as fertilizer.

A student in Freeburg, Illinois, tosses her waste into a recycling bin. She is participating in her school's recycling program.

Illinois has a long way to go before it solves its solid-waste problem. The state will eventually run out of room in its landfills. But if everyone works to reduce and recycle, Illinois will be able to handle its waste further into the future.

ALL ABOUT ILLINOIS

Fun Facts

The people of Metropolis, Illinois, claim that their town is the home of the legendary Superman. Pictures of the cartoon character appear on the town's water tower and on a billboard at the town's entrance. From the city's official Superman phone booth you can even talk to Superman!

Western Avenue in Chicago is the longest continuous city street in the world—it goes on for 24.5 miles.

Chicago's Sears Tower is one of the tallest buildings in the world. Completed in 1973, it's 1,454 feet, or about one-fourth of a mile high, and has 110 stories.

Squirrels live in most cities in Illinois. But the town of Olney is home to many white squirrels. In 1902 a boy named Thomas Tippitt set free a pair of the unusual animals. The male was killed, but the female soon appeared with babies. The white squirrel population has grown into the hundreds.

Olney protects the squirrels with special laws. White squirrels always have the right of way on streets in Olney, and no one may take a white squirrel out of town. The city's flag bears a white squirrel, and police cars have pictures of squirrels on their doors.

YOU ARE NOW LEAVING OLNEY

STATE SONG

The words to the Illinois state song were written in 1893. The music comes from a popular song called "Baby Mine," which was written in 1875. "Illinois" was adopted as the official state song in 1925.

ILLINOIS

Words by C. H. Chamberlain; music by Archibald Johnston

By thy riv-ers gen-tly flow-ing, Il - li - nois, Il - li-nois, O'er thy

prai-ries ver-dant grow-ing, Il - li - nois, Il - li-nois, Comes an ech-o on the breeze, Rus-tling

thro the leaf-y trees, and its mel-low tones are these, Il - li -

nois, Il - li-nois, And its mel-low tones are these, Il - li - nois!

You can hear Illinois's state song by visiting this website:
<http://www.state.il.us/state/sound/default.htm>

AN ILLINOIS RECIPE

Throughout the 1900s, Chicago was a center for Polish immigration. Pierogies are a staple of Polish food, and dozens of Chicago restaurants serve them. Pierogies can be filled with almost anything. This recipe uses potatoes and cheese.

PIEROGIES

For the dough:
2 cups flour
1 teaspoon salt
¼ teaspoon baking powder
1 egg

For the filling:
4 medium potatoes, cooked and mashed
¼ teaspoon salt
½ cup grated sharp cheese

To make the dough:
1. Mix together flour, salt, baking powder, and egg.
2. On a floured surface, knead dough for about 5 minutes.
3. Let dough sit for 10 minutes.
4. Roll out dough so that it is very thin, and cut into two-inch squares.

To make the filling:
1. Boil potatoes until they are soft, 15–20 minutes.
2. Mash them in a bowl and mix with cheese and salt.

Put a spoonful of filling on each of the dough squares. Fold them in half so that they make little triangles, and pinch the edges together. Boil until they bob to the surface of the water (about five minutes), and then drain. You can eat them as they are or fry them. Serve the pierogies with tomato sauce, sour cream, butter, or sauerkraut.

HISTORICAL TIMELINE

10,000 B.C. People first arrive in what later became Illinois.

300 B.C. Mound builders settle in Illinois.

A.D. 1400 The mound builders' city of Cahokia is deserted.

1673 Louis Jolliet and Jacques Marquette travel up the Illinois River.

1779 Du Sable builds the settlement that would later become Chicago.

1809 Illinois becomes a U.S. territory.

1818 Illinois becomes the 21st state.

1832 The Black Hawk War, the last major conflict between Native Americans and European settlers in Illinois, is fought.

1837 John Deere develops a steel plow in Grand Detour.

1848 The Illinois and Michigan Canal opens, connecting Lake Michigan to the Illinois and Mississippi Rivers.

1854 Senator Stephen Douglas introduces the Kansas-Nebraska Act.

1871 The Great Chicago Fire destroys parts of Chicago.

1886 The Haymarket Riot breaks out during a labor strike.

1908 Racial tension leads to rioting in Springfield.

1929 A battle between rival gangsters, known as the Saint Valentine's Day massacre, results in several deaths.

1937 The Great Flood of the Ohio River strikes Illinois.

1971 Illinois adopts a new state constitution.

1983 Chicagoans elect Howard Washington as their first black mayor.

1993 Floods damage many towns and farms in southern Illinois.

1998 The Chicago Bulls win their sixth NBA championship in eight seasons.

2001 Census data show that, by population, Chicago remained the third-largest U.S. city.

OUTSTANDING ILLINOISANS

Jane Addams

Jane Addams (1860–1935), a social worker born in Cedarville, Illinois, founded Hull-House with a friend in 1889. The settlement house provided child care, classes for children and adults, and other services for the immigrant families who lived in Chicago's slums. Addams created the first playground in Chicago and won the Nobel Peace Prize in 1931.

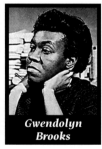

Philip Armour

Philip Armour (1832–1901) started Armour and Company, a huge meat-packing operation, in Chicago. He was known for making his meat products out of "every part of the pig but the squeal."

Ida B. Wells-Barnett (1862–1931) was a journalist and activist who moved to Chicago in 1893. She wrote editorials and made speeches about the rights of both women and African Americans. She started the country's first group for black women seeking the right to vote.

Gwendolyn Brooks

Gwendolyn Brooks (1917–2000), a writer, grew up in Chicago. In 1950 she won a Pulitzer Prize for *Annie Allen,* a book of poems. Brooks was named the poet laureate (outstanding poet) of Illinois. She was also the first African American to win the Pulitzer.

Al Capone (1899–1947) moved from New York to Chicago in 1919. He was soon in charge of a gang of criminals. He controlled the gambling and the supply of liquor in the city, and his gang often got into bloody gunfights with other gangs. In 1931 he went to prison for cheating on his taxes.

Al Capone

Richard J. Daley (1902–1976) was the mayor of Chicago from 1955 until his death. He was famous for his complete control of Chicago's government. He rewarded his supporters with jobs and kept his enemies from gaining power.

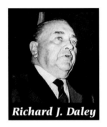

Richard J. Daley

David Davis (1815–1886) was a Supreme Court justice from 1862 to 1877. As a circuit court judge in Illinois, Davis helped secure Abraham Lincoln's presidential nomination in 1860. He ran for president himself as the Labor Reform Party candidate in 1872.

Miles Davis (1926–1990) was born in Alton, Illinois. A trumpet player, he recorded famous albums such as *Kind of Blue* and *Miles Ahead*. Davis played a major role in creating new styles of jazz after the 1940s.

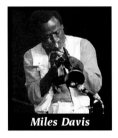

Miles Davis

Stephen A. Douglas (1813–1861) represented Illinois in the U.S. House of Representatives and the U.S. Senate for 17 years. He ran for U.S. president in 1860 but was defeated by Abraham Lincoln.

Roger Ebert (born 1942) is a film critic from Urbana, Illinois. In 1975 he became the first film critic to win the Pulitzer Prize for criticism. In addition to working on television in "Ebert & Roeper and the Movies," he writes about film for the *Chicago Sun-Times*.

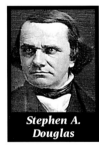

Stephen A. Douglas

Enrico Fermi (1901–1954) was a scientist who came to the United States from Italy in 1938, the year he won a Nobel Prize in physics. At the University of Chicago, he and his team of scientists learned how to release nuclear energy, which made the development of the nuclear bomb possible.

George Ferris (1859–1896), of Galesburg, Illinois, built the world's largest "pleasure wheel" in 1893. It was 250 feet high. The pleasure wheels soon became known as Ferris wheels in honor of Ferris.

Enrico Fermi

Harrison Ford

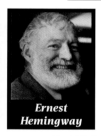
Benny Goodman

Ernest Hemingway

Mahalia Jackson

Marshall Field (1834–1906) moved to Chicago when he was 22. There, he founded Marshall Field & Company, a department store. He was the first store owner in the country to allow unhappy customers to exchange their purchases.

Harrison Ford (born 1942) played Han Solo in three *Star Wars* movies. The actor's other films include *Air Force One* and three *Indiana Jones* movies. Ford is from Chicago.

Benny Goodman (1909–1986), a jazz clarinet player and a bandleader, is known as the King of Swing. Goodman, who was a Chicagoan, won a Grammy Award for his life achievement in music in 1985.

Ernest Hemingway (1899–1961), a famous and influential writer, was born in Oak Park. He is remembered for books including *The Sun Also Rises*, *Farewell to Arms*, and *For Whom the Bell Tolls*. He won a Pulitzer Prize for *The Old Man and the Sea* in 1952. He won the Nobel Prize for literature in 1954.

Mahalia Jackson (1911–1972) moved to Chicago at the age of 15 and started her career as a gospel singer one year later. Her albums and concerts helped make gospel music popular throughout the country. She also worked to gain equal rights for African Americans.

Ray A. Kroc (1902–1984) bought a small fast-food restaurant called McDonald's from two Californians in the 1950s. Kroc reopened McDonald's in Des Plaines, Illinois, and turned it into a chain of restaurants, which have expanded throughout the world.

Abraham Lincoln (1809–1865) started his career as a politician in New Salem, Illinois, and later practiced law in Springfield. He became U.S. president in 1861 and freed the slaves in the Southern states during the Civil War one year later.

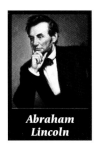

Abraham Lincoln

Richard Pryor (born 1940), from Peoria, has acted in many films, including *Stir Crazy.* But Pryor is probably best known as a stand-up comic and has won five Grammy Awards for his comedy albums.

Ronald Reagan (born 1911) served as U.S. president from 1981 until 1989. Born in Tampico, he left Illinois after college for California to start a successful film and television acting career. He went on to be governor of California for two terms.

Richard Pryor

Carl Sandburg (1878–1967) was a writer and poet who grew up in Galesburg. His writing dealt with American, especially Midwestern, themes. He is known for his biography of Abraham Lincoln, for the Pulitzer Prize–winning *Complete Poems,* for *Rootabaga Stories,* and for two other books for children.

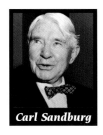

Carl Sandburg

Shel Silverstein (1932–1999), born and raised in Chicago, was an author, cartoonist, and composer. Silverstein's writing and drawings are featured in his popular books *Where the Sidewalk Ends, A Light in the Attic, Lafcadio the Lion,* and *The Giving Tree.*

Robin Williams (born 1952), from Chicago, has acted in many movies, including *Good Morning, Vietnam; Dead Poets Society;* and *Bicentennial Man.* He won an Oscar for best supporting actor for his role in *Good Will Hunting.* Williams also played Mork on the television show "Mork and Mindy."

Robin Williams

FACTS-AT-A-GLANCE

Nickname: Prairie State

Song: "Illinois"

Motto: State Sovereignty, National Union

Slogan: Land of Lincoln

Flower: native violet

Tree: white oak

Bird: cardinal

Animal: white-tailed deer

Fish: bluegill

Insect: monarch butterfly

Fossil: Tully monster

Date and ranking of statehood:
    December 3, 1818, the 21st state

Capital: Springfield

Area: 55,593 square miles

Rank in area, nationwide: 24th

Average January temperature: 26° F

Average July temperature: 76° F

The state flag of Illinois shows an eagle sitting on a boulder in a prairie. A banner imprinted with the state motto flies from the eagle's beak. The flag also shows two dates, 1818, the year Illinois became a state, and 1868, the year the state seal was chosen.

POPULATION GROWTH

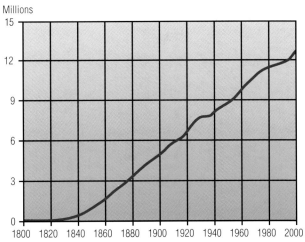

Millions

This chart shows how Illinois's population has grown from 1800 to 2000.

Population: 12,419,293 (2000 census)

Rank in population, nationwide: 5th

Major cities and populations: (2000 census) Chicago (2,896,016), Rockford (150,115), Aurora (142,990), Naperville (128,358), Peoria (112,936)

U.S. senators: 2

U.S. representatives: 19

Electoral votes: 21

Natural resources: clay, coal, fluorspar, gravel, limestone, oil, peat, sand, soil

Agricultural products: apples, barley, beef cattle, corn, flowers, hay, hogs, milk, sorghum, soybeans, wheat

Manufactured goods: cars, chemicals, construction equipment, electrical equipment, farm machinery, food products, machine tools, medicines, newspapers and books, transportation equipment

The state seal of Illinois was adopted in 1868. It appears on the flag as well as on official state documents.

WHERE ILLINOISANS WORK

Services—67 percent (services includes jobs in trade; community, social, and personal services; finance, insurance, and real estate; transportation, communication, and utilities)

Manufacturing—14 percent

Government—12 percent

Construction—5 percent

Agriculture—2 percent

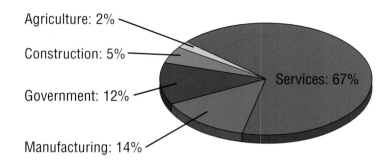

Agriculture: 2%
Construction: 5%
Government: 12%
Manufacturing: 14%
Services: 67%

GROSS STATE PRODUCT

Services—65 percent

Manufacturing—19 percent

Government—10 percent

Construction—4 percent

Agriculture—2 percent

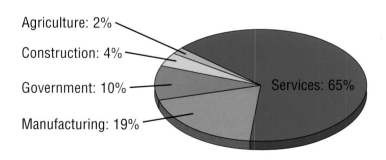

Agriculture: 2%
Construction: 4%
Government: 10%
Manufacturing: 19%
Services: 65%

ILLINOIS WILDLIFE

Mammals: beaver, deer, fox, muskrat, opossum, rabbit, raccoon, skunk, squirrel

Birds: Canada goose, duck, pheasant, quail

Reptiles and amphibians: dusky salamander, Illinois mud turtle, river cooter

Fish: bass, bigeye chub, carp, greater red-horse, perch, pike, pugnose shiner, sunfish

Trees: cottonwood, maple, oak, walnut

Wild plants: bloodroot, cuckooflower, squirting cucumber, toothwort, water pennywort, wild lettuce, woolly milkweed

River cooter

PLACES TO VISIT

Art Institute of Chicago
This world-renowned art museum has a fine collection of
Impressionist paintings as well as exhibits on Asian art, American
art, history, and more. It holds some of the most famous works
of art, including Grant Wood's *American Gothic* and Georges
Seurat's *Sunday Afternoon on the Island of La Grande Jatte.*

Brookfield Zoo
Nearly 2,300 animals inhabit this 216-acre zoo, which is
known all over the world for its nature exhibits and
conservation efforts.

Cahokia Mounds State Historic Site, near Collinsville
Visitors can learn about the mound builders of prehistoric
Illinois by taking a hike through the mounds and a visit to the
on-site Cahokia Mounds Interpretive Center.

Illinois State Museum, Springfield
The main branch of this museum focuses on the natural and
cultural history of Illinois. Its four other branches, located
throughout the state, house exhibits on Illinois's art and
archeology.

Lincoln's Home National Historic Site, Springfield
Guides lead tours of the home in which Abraham Lincoln and
his family lived from 1844 until 1861.

Lincoln's New Salem State Historic Site, near Petersburg
Visitors can explore this re-creation of the frontier village in which Abraham Lincoln lived during the 1830s. Lincoln began his political career in New Salem.

McDonald's #1 Store Museum, Des Plaines
This museum takes the form of a reproduction of the original McDonald's Restaurant, which opened in 1955. The site was built according to the original restaurant's blueprints.

Museum of Science and Industry, Chicago
Science and technology are explored in fun and fascinating ways at this museum, which is famed for its hands-on exhibits. Tourists can visit a coal mine, a captured World War II German submarine, and a chicken hatchery.

Sears Tower Skydeck, Chicago
From the 103rd floor of one of the world's tallest buildings, visitors can see all the way to Indiana, Michigan, and Wisconsin. The elevator takes one minute to zoom from the ground floor to the skydeck.

Ulysses S. Grant Home State Historic Site, Galena
President Ulysses S. Grant lived in this house when he was away from Washington, D.C., from 1865 until 1880.

Sears Tower

ANNUAL EVENTS

Saint Patrick's Day Parade, Chicago—*March*

Old Capitol Art Fair, Springfield—*May*

Steamboat Days and Race, Peoria—*June*

Taste of Chicago—*June–July*

Ravinia Festival, Highland Park—*June–September*

Venetian Night, Chicago—*July*

Mendota Sweet Corn Festival, Mendota—*August*

Du Quoin State Fair and World Trotting Derby, Du Quoin—*August or September*

Chicago Jazz Festival—*August–September*

Illinois State Fair, Springfield—*September*

Pumpkin Festival, Sycamore—*October*

International Folk Fair, Chicago—*November*

LEARN MORE ABOUT ILLINOIS

BOOKS

General

Fradin, Dennis Brindell. *Illinois.* Chicago: Children's Press, 1994.

Santella, Andrew, and Stein, Conrad R. *Illinois.* Chicago: Children's Press, 1998. For older readers.

Wills, Charles A. *A Historical Album of Illinois.* Brookfield, CT: Millbrook Press, 1994. For older readers.

Special Interest

Arnold, Caroline. *Children of the Settlement Houses.* Minneapolis: Carolrhoda Books, Inc., 1998. Historical photos and text explain the role of settlement, or community, houses in big cities in the late 1800s and early 1900s. Discusses Chicago's Hull-House.

Bial, Raymond. *Portrait of a Farm Family.* Boston: Houghton-Mifflin, 1995. Through text and photographs, Bial presents one family's life on dairy farm in rural Illinois.

Harness, Cheryl. *Young Abe Lincoln: The Frontier Days, 1809–1837.* Washington, D.C.: National Geographic, 1996. This picture book traces Abraham Lincoln's early years through three states, many occupations, and family tragedies until he settles as a lawyer in Springfield, Illinois.

Murphy, Jim. *The Great Fire.* New York: Scholastic, 1995. This account of the three-day blaze that left 100,000 Chicagoans homeless features personal accounts and period photographs. A Newbery Honor Book in 1996.

Raber, Thomas. *Michael Jordan: Basketball Skywalker.* Minneapolis: Lerner Publications/LernerSports, 1999. The life story of the superstar basketball player who led the Chicago Bulls to victory during the 1990s.

Toht, David W. *Sodbuster.* Minneapolis: Lerner Publications, 1996. This fully illustrated exploration of day-to-day farm life between 1800 and 1850 focuses on Illinois and other Midwestern states.

Welch, Catherine A. *Ida B. Wells-Barnett: Powerhouse with a Pen.* Minneapolis: Carolrhoda Books, Inc., 2000. Welch shares the story of the journalist and activist and her efforts to end lynching. Illustrated with historical photographs.

Fiction

Peck, Richard. *A Long Way From Chicago.* New York: Dial Books, 1998. Peck chronicles nine yearly visits to a rural Illinois town during the 1920s and 1930s. Each year, their grandmother involves Joey and Mary Alice in new schemes and adventures. A Newbery Honor Book in 1999.

Robinet, Harriette Gillem. *Children of the Fire.* New York: Simon and Schuster, 1991. Eleven-year-old Hallelujah's experiences during and after the Chicago fire teach her new tolerance. The daughter of an escaped slave, Hallelujah learns that all people are equals when disaster strikes.

WEBSITES

State of Illinois
<http://state.il.us/>
The official website of the state of Illinois. A special section of the site, called Kid Zone, is geared to the interests of young people.

Illinois Tourism
<http://www.state.il.us/state/tourism>
Plan your trips to the parks, museums, historical sites, festivals, and other attractions of Illinois by visiting this website.

Chicago Tribune
<http://chicagotribune.com>
Read about current events in the online version of this popular Illinois newspaper.

PRONUNCIATION GUIDE

Cahokia (kuh-HOH-kee-uh)

du Sable, Jean Baptiste Point (doo SAH-bleh, zhawn bah-teest pwah)

Galena (guh-LEE-nuh)

Illinois (ihl-uh-NOY)

Jolliet, Louis (JOH-lee-ay, LOO-ihs)

Kaskaskia (ka-SKAS-kee-uh)

Marquette, Jacques (mahr-KEHT, zhahk)

Peoria (pee-OHR-ee-uh)

Potawatomi (paht-uh-WHAT-uh-mee)

Sauk (SAWK)

Wabash (WAH-bash)

GLOSSARY

glacier: a large body of ice and snow that moves slowly over land

Great Lakes: a chain of five lakes in Canada and the northern United States. They are Lakes Superior, Michigan, Huron, Erie, and Ontario.

groundwater: water that lies beneath the earth's surface. The water comes from rain and snow that seep through soil into the cracks and other openings in rocks. Groundwater supplies wells and springs.

immigrant: a person who moves into a foreign country and settles there

landfill: a place specially prepared for burying solid waste

leachate: liquid that has seeped through waste or that forms when waste rots in a landfill. Leachate can contaminate water or soil.

prairie: a large area of level or gently rolling grassy land with few trees

solid waste: useless or unwanted solid and semisolid materials that have been thrown away. Solid waste includes dry waste, food waste, yard waste, ashes, industrial waste, appliances, furniture, and construction waste.

speakeasy: a place where alcoholic beverages are sold illegally

INDEX

PHOTO ACKNOWLEDGMENTS

Cover photographs by © Ron Watts/CORBIS (right) and © Richard Hamilton Smith/CORBIS (left); Digital Cartographics, pp. 1, 8, 9, 44; David Muench/Corbis, pp. 2–3; Lee Snider/Corbis, p. 3; © Howard Ande, pp. 4 (detail), 6, 7 (detail), 17 (detail), 40 (detail), 52 (detail); Illinois Department of Commerce and Community Affairs, pp. 7, 12, 40, 47, 49 (bottom), 50 (top); Kent & Donna Dannen, p. 10; Scott Berner/Visuals Unlimited, p. 11; Gail Nachel/Root Resources, p. 13; Martin J. Schmidt/Root Resources, p. 14; Phyllis Cerny, pp. 15, 42; Alan G. Nelson/Root Resources, p. 16; Loren M. Root/Root Resources, p. 17; Cahokia Mounds State Historic Site, p. 18; Illinois State Historical Library, pp. 19, 26, 66 (bottom), 67 (top), 68 (second from top); Missouri Historical Society, J.N. Marchland (neg. Events 4a), p. 21; Chicago Historical Society, pp. 22, 31, 36; Independent Picture Service, pp. 24, 66 (second from bottom); Deere & Company, pp. 25, 45; Lake County (IL) Museum, Regional History Archives, p. 27; Library of Congress, pp. 28, 29, 30, 32, 35, 37, 38, 67 (second from bottom); Lake County (IL) Museum, Curt Teich Postcard Archives, p. 33 (both); UPI/Bettman Newsphotos/CORBIS, p. 39; © Sandy Felsenthal/CORBIS, p. 41; Terry Farmer, pp. 43, 81; Irene Z. Meyers/Root Resources, p. 46; © Joseph Sohm/CORBIS, p. 48; The Time Museum, Rockford, Illinois, p. 49 (top); Kevin Horan, Kohl Children's Museum, Wilmette, IL, p. 50 (bottom); © Kim Karpeles, p. 51; Tom Hecht/Illinois Department of Energy and Natural Resources (ENR), Springfield, Illinois, p. 52; © Ned Axthelm, IPS, p. 53; Jerry Boucher, pp. 54, 56, 58; Southern Illinois Tourism Council, p. 57; Robert Tyszka © 1992, p. 59; Metropolis Planet Photo, p. 60; Jack Lindstrom, p. 61; Tim Seeley, pp. 63, 71, 72; Minneapolis Public Library and Information Center, pp. 66 (top), 69 (top); Armour and Company, p. 66 (second from top); CBS Records, p. 67 (second from top); University of Chicago, p. 67 (bottom); Hollywood Book and Poster, Inc., pp. 68 (top), 69 (second from top); Popperfoto/Archive Photos, pp. 68 (second from bottom), 69 (second from bottom); Station KSTP – Minneapolis, p. 68 (bottom); Photofest, p. 69 (bottom); Jean Matheny, p. 70; © Eric and David Hosking/CORBIS, p. 73; © Angelo Hornak/CORBIS, p. 75; City of Chicago, Mayor Richard M. Daley, p. 80.